Twenty-Two Splendid Tales To Tell from Around the World
Volume Two

Twenty-Two Splendid Tales to Tell From Around the World
Volume Two

Pleasant DeSpain

Illustrated by Kirk Lyttle

August House Publishers, Inc.
LITTLE ROCK

Printed in the United States of America

10 9 8 7 6 5 4 3 2 1

LIBRARY OF CONGRESS CATALOGING-IN-PUBLICATION DATA

DeSpain, Pleasant.
Twenty-two splendid tales to tell from around the world/
Pleasant DeSpain; illustrated by Kirk Lyttle. — [3rd ed.]
p.   cm.
Previously published as: Pleasant Journeys, v. 1-2.
Summary: An illustrated collection of traditional tales from Europe,
Asia, Africa, and the Americas. Includes brief notes for storytellers.
ISBN 0-87483-340-X (v. 1 : alk. paper) : $11.95
ISBN 0-87483-341-8 (v. 2 : alk. paper) : $11.95
1. Tales. [1. Folklore.] I. Lyttle, Kirk, ill.   II. DeSpain, Pleasant.
Pleasant Journeys. III. Title.
PZ8.1.D47Tw   1994
398.2—dc20   94-1020

Executive editor: Liz Parkhurst
Project editor: Rufus Griscom
Design director: Ted Parkhurst
Cover design: Wendall Hall
Illustrations: Kirk Lyttle
Author photograph: Greg Nystrom

AUGUST HOUSE, INC.   PUBLISHERS   LITTLE ROCK

for Robert A. DeSpain, my father,
and in loving memory of Rose DeSpain, my stepmother

Contents

Preface

The twenty-two stories in this second volume of Splendid Tales to Tell are my versions of traditional folk tales representing sixteen different countries and cultures. Like those in Volume One, these were originally published in "Pleasant Journeys," my weekly column in *The Seattle Times*. They are "tellable" tales, and I have enjoyed sharing them with children of all ages.

During my visits to hundreds of elementary schools over the years, I've met thousands of great kids. And many of them have asked me the same question: "What is your favorite story?"

This is a difficult question to answer. It's impossible for me to have one or two or even ten favorites. I like all the stories that I tell, and I'm a lucky man because I get to tell as many as I want.

The tales in this collection are just some of my favorites. I hope that you will like them too, and that you will learn some of them to tell to your friends.

Acknowledgments

I am fortunate to have such good and willing friends and colleagues. I wish to thank the following for their valued help and encouragement in bringing forth all three editions of these tales to tell: Leslie Gillian Abel, Merle and Anne Dowd, Edward Edelstein, Rufus Griscom, Robert Guy, Daniel Higgins, Roger Lanphear, Kirk Lyttle, Ted and Liz Parkhurst, Lynn Rubright, Ruthmarie Arguello-Sheehan, Mason Sizemore, Perrin Stifel, Paul Thompson, and T.R. Welch.

Introduction to the Third Edition

It is with pleasure that I introduce the third edition of this collection of tellable tales. Since their initial publication as *Pleasant Journeys* in 1979, many delightful stories have come my way from readers and tellers about their own funny, beautiful, and unexpected experiences with these tales. It's reassuring to discover that our stories of old retain their energy, wisdom, and simple fun in these complicated times.

Hopefully, you'll find an improved book in this edition. The covers are more appealing, the stories are more closely edited, and I have provided new source notes and storytelling tips.

I'm profoundly grateful to all the storytellers who have found these tales worthy of sharing. With all the tellers who are discovering them for the first time, I wish to share a fundamental belief: you can and will accomplish amazing things with the power of your voice, telling a story you love to listeners you care about. Trust yourself, trust the story, and most of all, trust your listeners.

The world will always need more storytellers …

—Pleasant DeSpain
Seattle, Washington

The Extraordinary Cat
A Chinese Tale

Once there was a Chinese ruler who had a cat that he treasured above all other animals. He loved the cat so much and thought that it was so extraordinary that he named it Sky.

One day soon after, an advisor to the court spoke to the ruler and explained, "There is something much more powerful than the sky, and that is the cloud. The cloud can darken and even hide the sky from view."

"Quite right," agreed the ruler. "From this day forth, my beautiful cat shall be called Cloud."

Two weeks later the ruler's wife said, "Dear husband, I don't think that Cloud is a proper name for your cat. There is something stronger than the cloud, and that is the wind that blows the cloud about."

"Indeed! From now on my superior cat will be called Wind. Here Wind! Here Wind! Nice little Wind."

During the next month, the ruler's brother came for a visit and agreed that the cat was the most extraordinary animal he had ever seen. "But," he said, "Wind is not a suitable name for this superb creature. The wind is servant to that which it cannot penetrate ... such as a wall. The wall is stronger than the wind."

"I hadn't thought of that," replied the ruler, "and you are to be congratulated, brother, for being so observant. From now on, my dearest cat, the most wonderful cat on earth, will be called Wall."

The very next day the royal gardener heard the ruler call his cat, "Wall," and said, "But sire, you are forgetting that a mouse is able to chew a hole in a wall. The mouse is the strongest."

"How clever of you," said the ruler. "From this day forth, my lovely cat will be called Mouse. Come here Mouse!"

But just then the ruler's boy and girl skipped into the garden to play, and when they heard their father call the cat, "Mouse," they started to laugh and laugh!

"What causes you to laugh, children?" asked the ruler.

"Father," replied the little girl, "everyone knows that there is something stronger than the mouse, and that's the cat who catches it!"

The ruler smiled as he realized that his children were the wisest of all his advisors. Then he began to laugh. "Of course! How foolish I've been. From now on my extraordinary animal will be called by the name he most deserves, and that is Cat!"

The Proud Fox
An American Tale

Once upon a time, a proud fox was taking a leisurely walk through the forest when a pack of wild dogs caught his scent and started to chase after him, yelping and howling as they ran. The fox knew that he was the fastest runner in the land and enjoyed the prospect of outwitting the dogs as he had before. He leaped into the air and bounded through the forest towards his den.

But the dogs were larger than the fox and nearly as swift, and they were able to cut off his path to the den and force him to run back out of the woods towards the open plains. The fox ran even harder and faster, but the dogs were strong and began to gain on him. Now he was running for his life and he looked desperately for a place to hide!

The plains were vast and he was surrounded by open space. The pack of dogs was howling wildly and they were so close that they were nipping at his bushy tail! Just then the fox saw a small cave in a large pile of boulders and headed straight for it. The dogs stayed with him and very nearly caught him, but the fox bounded through the rocks and dove into the dark cave!

Fortunately the cave was small—too small for the dogs to enter. They barked and whined and pawed at the ground, but soon they quieted down and all was still.

Now that the fox was safe, he began to feel quite proud of himself once again. He wanted to boast of his skillful run, but there was no one in the cave to listen to him. So he began a conversation with the separate parts of his body.

"Feet, what did you do to help me win the race?" asked the fox.

"We leaped into the air and carried you ahead of those mean dogs," said his feet. "We ran faster than ever before and brought you to this cave."

"Excellent! You are good feet and I'm proud of all of you. Now, ears, what was your role?"

"We heard the dogs coming and told the feet to start running," replied the ears.

"Very well done!" said the fox. "And now, my eyes. What did you do to help?"

"We found the path to follow. We looked to the right and to the left, and we saw this cave in the rocks."

"Wonderful! Just wonderful! What a splendid fox I am to have such excellent feet, ears, and eyes!"

"Ah-hem," said the tail, "aren't you forgetting me?"

"Oh yes," said the fox, "how could I forget you, my friendly tail? After all, wasn't it you who almost got me caught by letting the dogs nip at the end of you? Or did you help in some other way that I'm not aware of?"

That made the tail so angry that it said, "I also helped by waving in the air, urging the dogs forward so that they could catch you!"

"Enough!" cried the fox. "How dare you mock me! You are not brave like the others. You are a coward and do not belong in the safety of this cave with the rest of us! Outside with you, traitor! Out! Out you go!"

And the fox backed his tail out of the cave's entrance. The dogs, who were hidden in the rocks, immediately pounced upon it, and that was the end of the proud fox.

The Wisdom of Solomon
An Israeli Tale

Once during the reign of the wise King Solomon, the Queen of Sheba traveled from her palace to meet with him. She brought with her one thousand soldiers, craftsmen, and attendants, as well as the most wonderful treasures of her kingdom.

Her artisans had created objects of wonder and delight such as had never before been seen! There were birds of gold and silver that could fly about the room and sing as beautifully as living birds; a clock made of wood so rare that it recorded the time of the past, present, and future; and a carpet woven from the manes of flying horses—a carpet that could fly!

King Solomon looked upon these things and with a calm voice said, "These are works of genius."

The Queen of Sheba clapped her hands and her attendants carried in two vases of flowers and placed them before the King. Then she spoke for all to hear:

"O wise and noble Solomon, greatest ruler in all the world, I bring these treasures to you as gifts from my small kingdom. They are to make you smile when your heart grows heavy.

Now before you rest two vases of flowers which appear to be identical, but only one consists of living flowers. The other is a copy made from gold leaf, precious gems, and brightly colored enamels. Thus I put the following test to the wisest of all living men: which is the true and which is the false?"

Solomon realized that this was no mere game. It was a serious challenge to his reputation as the wisest of kings. If he chose the wrong one, all the world would know of his failure and his glory would be lost.

He gazed upon the wondrous beauty of the flowers, seeking the imperfections that would reveal the false bouquet. The lilies in both vases were perfectly matched, as were the roses and the other blossoms, and each stem wore bright green leaves.

He searched until he discovered a transparent drop of dew on a red rose petal and was about to point his finger to the vase which contained it and say, "These are the flowers grown in nature's garden," but just then he saw an identical dew drop on the same petal in the second vase.

Solomon sat quietly and puzzled over the riddle as everyone in court awaited his answer. Just then a bee from his garden flew in through one of the open windows. A guard started after it, but Solomon quickly said, "Do not harm our little friend. Let him alight where he will."

Flying undeterred, the bee soon approached the two vases of flowers. Solomon smiled, realizing that the insect would not be fooled by the artisan's skill nor by gold, jewels, and false color. Without hesitation the bee landed on the garden flowers. Solomon raised his hand and pointed to the same bouquet.

The Queen of Sheba bowed before him respectfully, for she too realized that nature is the wisest of all teachers, and even if it is only a bee sent to instruct, it is the wise who listen.

The Bear Who Said North
A Finnish Tale

Once upon a time, long, long ago, a lumbering, clumsy old bear caught a fat grouse. The bear was so proud of his achievement that he held the frightened bird with his teeth, being very careful not to harm it. This way he could walk through the forest showing all the other animals that he wasn't such a foolish bear after all.

"The others say I'm just a silly old bear, but when they see that I've caught this fine fat bird they will change their tune," he thought.

He began his proud walk along a heavily traveled forest trail and found the clever fox napping in the shade of a pine tree.

"Umph! Umph!" grunted the bear, trying to attract the fox's attention.

"Oh, go growl to the squirrels, you inconsiderate old fool. Can't you see that I'm having a sweet dream?" complained the fox.

"Umgh! Umgh!" the bear grunted even louder, for he especially wanted the fox to see his triumph.

The fox barely opened one eye and saw that his old enemy was showing off.

This made him even more angry, and he decided to play a trick on the bear for disturbing his nap. He yawned and opened his eyes, but he didn't look up at the bear. Instead, he pointed his nose to the ground and sniffed two or three times, being careful not to see the grouse caught in the bear's teeth.

"Tell me, friend," said the fox, "which way is the wind blowing just now?"

The bear couldn't answer without opening his mouth, and if he opened his mouth, the bird would fly away.

"Umph!" he grunted again, hoping that the fox would look up and see his captive.

"I believe it must be blowing from the west. Yes, it is blowing from the west, isn't that right, friend bear?"

"Umph! Umph! Umph!" said the bear, growing quite angry with the fox.

"What's that? You say it is from the west? But are you sure? Perhaps it is blowing from the south instead."

"Umph!" repeated the bear, growing more and more impatient with the fox.

"The south it is then, after all," said the fox. "But tell me, how did you figure it out?"

By now the bear was so exasperated with the fox that he momentarily forgot himself and opened his mouth to roar, "North! The wind is blowing from the north!"

The grouse flapped her wings the instant his mouth opened and flew to the safety of a high branch.

"Look at what you've made me do!" exclaimed the bear. "My fat bird has escaped and it's all your fault!"

"My fault?" asked the fox innocently.

"Why is it my fault?"

"Because you kept asking me about the direction of the wind until I had to open my mouth to answer!"

"But friend bear, why did you open your mouth to answer?" asked the fox.

"Because you can't say 'North!' without opening your mouth," said the unhappy bear.

The fox smiled and said, "If I had caught the grouse and you asked me the direction of the wind, I would not have answered 'North!'"

"Then what would you have said?" asked the bear.

The fox clenched his teeth together and said, "East!"

Toads and Diamonds
A French Tale

Once long ago, there lived a homely widow and her two daughters. The oldest girl looked just like her mother and was exceptionally ill-tempered. The youngest, however, was quite beautiful and had a sweet nature.

The mother favored the oldest daughter and made the youngest do all the housework. One of her daily tasks was to fetch a pail of water from the well in the forest which was over a mile from the cottage. One day, while she was at the well, a poor old woman came by and begged for a drink.

"Of course you shall have a drink," said the girl. "And I will hold the bucket up for you."

After drinking her fill, the old woman said, "I am a fairy in disguise. I wanted to see if your manners were a match for your beauty, and I'm happy to say that they are indeed. Thus I will give you a rare gift. With every word you speak, a rose or a precious diamond will fall from your pretty mouth."

When the youngest daughter returned from the well, her mother scolded her for being late.

"I am sorry, Mother, for taking so long." And as she spoke, two red roses and three sparkling diamonds came out of her mouth.

"What is the meaning of this?" demanded her mother.

The girl told the story of her encounter with the old woman and the mother said, "It is not you who deserves such a fine gift, it is your sister. Dearest," she called, for that is what she always called the elder daughter, "go to the well and draw a bucket of fresh water. When a poor old woman asks for a drink, be sure to give it to her."

"Fetching water is for servants and silly little sisters—it is not for the likes of me!"

"Go this instant," said her mother, "or you will find yourself chopping the firewood as well!"

Thus she went, grumbling all the way. When she reached the well, she saw a beautiful young woman in fine court dress coming out of the woods. This was the same fairy as before who had now taken the form of a princess.

"May I have a drink?" asked the fairy.

"I didn't walk all this way to serve the likes of you," said the unruly girl. "If you want a drink so badly, fetch it yourself!"

"You have but little in the way of manners," said the fairy. "My gift for you is that with every word you speak, a snake or a toad will spring from your rude mouth."

The girl ran home and called, "Mother, look at what has happened to me!" And so saying, two black snakes and three green toads leaped out of her mouth.

"It is your wicked sister who has

caused all of this!" exclaimed the mother. "And I shall beat her within an inch of her life!"

Upon overhearing the threat, the young girl ran from the house and hid in the deep forest. She knew that she could never return to the cottage again.

Just then a prince rode by on his way home from hunting and saw her among the trees. He noted that she looked frightened and asked the reason for her tears.

"It is my mother and sister," she explained. "They have driven me out."

The prince was already taken with her beauty, and when he saw the roses and diamonds fall from her mouth, he asked her to tell him all that had happened.

Upon hearing the story, he placed her on his horse, and they rode to the palace. Soon after, they were happily married.

The Shoemaker's Dream
A Dutch Tale

Once there was a poor old shoemaker who lived in a small country village, two days' walk from Amsterdam. He often dreamed of great wealth, but when he told his wife about his wonderful dreams, she only laughed and said, "We can't very well eat a dream—it won't fill our empty stomachs!"

One morning he awoke with a start and said, "Wife, I had a special dream last night. An angel came to me and said that I would find my fortune on the largest bridge in Amsterdam!"

"Nonsense," said his sleepy wife. "Dreams are not true, and you can't go off to the city when you have work here at home."

The next night he had the same dream, and the night after that it came again. Finally the shoemaker said, "I'm going to Amsterdam to find my fortune, wife, and nothing you can say will stop me."

It was a long and difficult journey, but at last the old man arrived in the city and went straight to the largest bridge. He walked across it slowly, searching for the treasure, but failed to find it. The bridge seemed quite ordinary and the people who crossed it were just like citizens anywhere. Again he walked across it, and again, but to no avail.

At last the shoemaker sat down on the railing, near the middle of the long expanse, and waited for something to happen. Soon it began to grow dark, and he sighed heavily knowing that he would have to begin his long journey home.

Just then a ragged beggar walked up to him and said, "Please excuse my boldness, but I've noticed that you've been looking for something on this bridge all day long. Perhaps I can help you find it."

"I doubt it," said the shoemaker. "I've had the same dream for three nights and that is why I've come all the way from my village to this very bridge in Amsterdam. I'm supposed to find my fortune right here."

"How strange," replied the beggar, "for I too have recently dreamed that I would find a chest filled with gold in the garden of a shoemaker who lives across the road from a small church, in a village two days' walk away from Amsterdam. But of course, I don't believe in dreams at all. Everyone knows that a dream can't fill an empty stomach." And with a smile the beggar walked away.

The shoemaker rushed home as fast as he could and, ignoring his wife's many questions, began digging up the garden. It wasn't long before he heard the dull thud of his hoe striking a metal chest. He unearthed it and dragged it into the house. The lock was old and full of rust and he had little difficulty breaking it open. The chest was filled to the top with shiny, gold coins!

With their fortune made, even the

shoemaker's wife had to agree that some-
times dreams can help to fill an empty
stomach.

The Bat
A Central Asian Tale

Once long ago, the bat did not sleep during the day and fly only at night as he does now. Instead he was wide awake during the daylight hours and he flew about the sky with all the birds.

One bright and sunny day he met an eagle winging his way across the sky.

"Friend Bat," called the eagle, "I have been searching everywhere for you."

"And what is it you want from me?" asked the bat.

"Your fair share of the taxes. All the other birds have paid theirs."

"I am not of the bird family," explained the bat. "Why should I pay if I am not a bird?"

"But you have wings and you fly like a bird," said the eagle. "We are flying together right now. Thus it is only fair that you pay too."

"Watch, friend Eagle, and I will prove to you that I am not a bird." And so saying, the bat flew to the ground and ran into the woods on four feet.

"He was right!" exclaimed the eagle. "He is not a bird. He is an animal!"

The bat soon came to a shady brook, and because he was tired from all of his running, stopped to rest.

Soon a thirsty tiger came to the stream to drink, and seeing the bat, said, "How glad I am to meet you at last, friend Bat. I've been looking for you for several months."

"For what reason?" asked the bat.

"Oh, a very important reason, I assure you," explained the tiger. "It seems that all the animals in the forest have paid their taxes. That is, all but you."

"I am not of the animal family," said the bat. "Why should I pay if I am not an animal?"

"But you walk on four feet just like all the other animals," replied the tiger, "so you must pay your share. It is only fair."

"Watch, friend Tiger, and I will prove to you that I am not an animal."

And so saying, the bat unfolded his wings and flew high into the air.

"It is true!" exclaimed the tiger. "The bat is not an animal after all. He is a bird!"

The bat didn't want to meet the tiger ever again, so he stopped using his small legs for walking, and soon they withered away. Nor did he fly during the daylight hours, since he didn't want to meet the eagle. Thus it is that he sleeps in dark caves by day and flies only at night, when the eagle rests.

The Seven Stars
A Native American (Cherokee) Tale

Long ago, when the world was young and the first forests were still growing, seven Indian boys played a game called wheel-and-spear.

Six of the boys stood behind a line made in the soft dirt and held their spears high. Then the seventh boy, whose name was Little Elk, rolled a small wheel made of stone across the grassy plain. The boys threw their spears at the wheel as it quickly rolled away from them, and the one who struck closest to it when it stopped was the winner.

"Ahh," cried Little Elk, "Gray Eagle wins! He has the highest score of all. Shall we try again?"

"Yes, once more!" said Gray Eagle happily.

The boys ran back to the throwing line, but before they could lift their spears, a loud voice came from one of the nearby lodges, "Gray Eagle! Enough of your foolish games! Come home for your supper or you will be punished!"

It was his mother. She was angry because Gray Eagle had played at the game each day for weeks.

Then Little Elk's mother came from

her lodge and grabbed her son by the arm, "You didn't catch any fish from the river. Instead you played at your silly game all afternoon. Now you will come home and there will be no supper for you tonight!"

Soon the other boys' mothers called them in too, and each was scolded for being late.

The next day the mothers met together to grind corn and discuss their problems.

"The boys spend too much time with their game," said Little Elk's mother. "My son has become lazy and neglects his chores. We must do something."

"You speak truthfully," said Gray Eagle's mother. "My son cares for nothing but the Wheel-and-Spear game. He is becoming a stranger to me. When he is home, he boasts of his skill at the game and talks of nothing else. We must end this foolishness."

All the other mothers agreed, and they decided upon a plan. Late that night while the boys slept, the mothers took their sons' stone wheels down to the river and dropped them into the deepest pool.

The boys were angry when they discovered what had happened and decided to run away.

"Come," said Little Elk to the others, "we will go to the field to dance and never again will we return."

"Yes," said Gray Eagle, "our mothers will not spoil our games ever again." The other boys agreed and then they formed a circle. Like swift-running deer they danced around the ring and chanted a simple song,

We will go far, we will go far.
No more to return, no more to return.

Around and around they sped, and instead of growing tired, they seemed to grow stronger. Faster they went, and faster yet, and soon their feet were no longer touching the earth.

Darkness began to fall, and the mothers came to the field in search of their dancing sons.

"Look!" cried Little Elk's mother. "They are rising into the air!"

"Quickly," yelled the mother of Gray Eagle, "grab their feet and pull them down!"

The women rushed toward their sons, but the boys were rising higher and higher with each circle. The mothers leaped as high as they could, grabbing for their sons' flying feet, but they could not reach them.

The dancing boys continued to rise until they reached the sky. Their mothers cried out and begged them to return, but it was of no use, for the boys turned into seven bright stars.

And if you look up at the heavens on a clear night, you can see them dancing still.

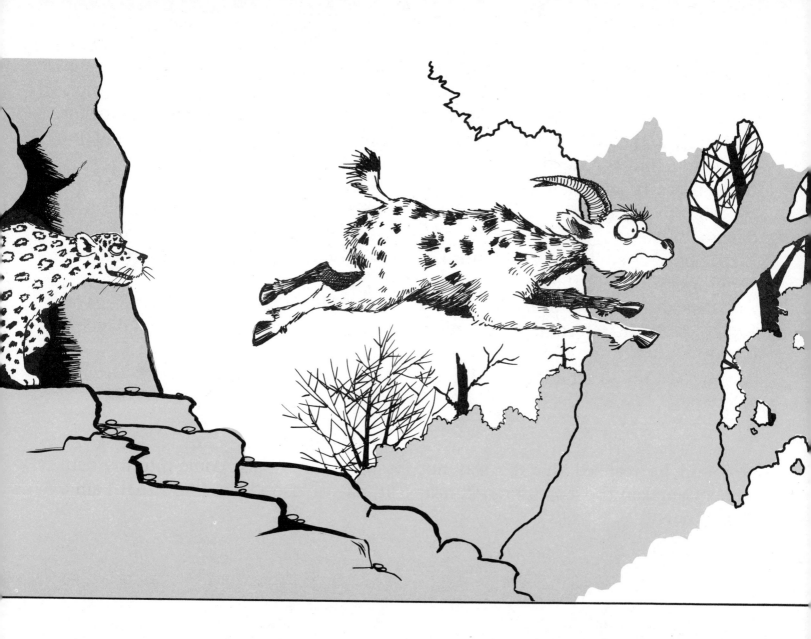

Josesito the Goat
A South American Tale

Once a goat named Josesito got caught in a raging rainstorm in the high mountains. Panic-stricken and seeking shelter, he ran until he came to a large dark cave. Josesito should have been cautious and checked to see if the cave was inhabited by anyone else, but instead he ran inside, shaking from the cold and wet.

Soon his eyes adjusted to the darkness and he realized that he was not alone. Cabrakan the leopard rested near the cave's entrance, pleased that his meal for the day had come so easily.

Josesito quickly realized that he would have to use whatever wit he could muster if he was to leave the cave in one piece. Thus he boldly lowered his head exposing the sharp tips of his curved horns.

Having recently eaten a small deer, the leopard was more curious than hungry and decided to have a chat with Josesito before killing him.

"Why have you come into my den, little Goat? Don't you know that I am a great hunter?"

"I sought shelter from the violent

storm," replied Josesito. "I didn't realize that this was your home. But since we are both hunters, I'm sure that you understand."

"You, a hunter?" asked the amused Cabrakan.

"I see that you do not believe me, friend Leopard. But it is true nonetheless. Yes, I hunt, but differently than you. I am only interested in the *sport* of hunting. I do not eat the flesh of the animals that I rip apart with my horns. My diet consists of green grass, spring flowers, fresh herbs, and whatever ripe fruit I can find. Meat is repugnant to me, but the hunt helps to keep up my strength and courage."

Josesito continued to stand in the darkest corner of the cave so that Cabrakan could not see that he shook from fear during the entire speech.

The leopard continued to be amused by this strange little goat and instead of pouncing on him, asked, "And what animal presents the greatest challenge when you hunt?"

"The puma, of course," replied Josesito, "for he is the most dangerous of all."

Cabrakan's smile quickly faded at the mention of his greatest enemy. "How is it that you hunt the powerful puma, Goat?" Cabrakan asked. "He is much larger and stronger than you."

"It is easy, my friend," said Josesito. "I lead him into a clearing and then lower my head and wait for him to spring. When he falls upon me, I quickly raise my head and pierce his heart with my sharp horns. I have killed many in this way."

Suddenly the storm was over and the goat realized that his game of daring was soon to end. He lowered his voice and attempted to sound sinister, "Now we will see who is the best hunter. Let's both go into the forest and make a kill. When the sun sets, we can return to the cave and compare our results."

"Agreed," said Cabrakan, whose smile had returned. He planned to stalk and kill the goat as soon as they left the dark recesses of the cave.

Then, with a surprising burst of speed, Josesito leaped for the cave's entrance and ran into the deep woods. The leopard was not alarmed since he knew that he would have little difficulty in catching up with him.

The goat ran through the trees and soon came to a small clearing. To his great surprise he saw a puma lying stretched out on the ground. It looked as though he had been killed in the storm, perhaps by a bolt of lightning. Seeing his opportunity, Josesito began to bleat loudly and butt the dead puma with his horns.

Cabrakan arrived a moment later and was shocked at what he saw! He turned and ran into the forest, and little Josesito never saw him again.

Three Children of Fortune
A German Tale

Once upon a time, a father gave his oldest son a rooster, his second son a scythe (a curved blade set into a long handle and used to cut grass or grain), and to his youngest son he gave a cat.

"I'm old and soon to die," he said, "and since I have no fortune to leave, you must take these gifts and try to make your own fortunes."

The oldest boy set out with his rooster and had to travel for three months to find a remote city in which a rooster had never been known. The townspeople in this city didn't even have clocks.

"Friends!" cried the youth. "Look upon my rooster and behold a miracle! Each morning he crows three times and tells me that the sun is soon to rise. And if he crows during the day, I know the weather is about to change."

The people were quite impressed and asked how much he would take for such a marvelous bird.

"As much gold as a donkey can carry," he replied.

And to that they agreed.

When the oldest boy returned home

with his treasure, it was time for the second son to leave with his scythe. He traveled for half a year before he came to a farming village in which the people had not yet seen nor heard of a scythe. When their wheat or corn was ready to be harvested they pulled it up from the ground by hand—roots and all. The work was hard and slow and much of the harvest was destroyed in the process.

The boy began to swing his scythe and soon an entire field was cut clean. The farmers were shocked and stood with open mouths. They were happy to give him as much gold as a horse could carry in exchange for the wonderful tool.

Upon the return of the second son, it was time for the youngest boy to take his cat into the wide world and seek his fortune. He traveled for a year and a day, but everywhere he wandered he found other cats.

Thus he booked passage on a ship and with his cat under his coat, sailed to far-off lands. At last he landed on a remote island where no one had ever heard of a cat. It was no surprise that the island was overrun with mice.

Even the king had no peace from the multitude of rodents that ran freely throughout the palace. They ate whatever they wanted and squeaked all day long. They took baths in the king's porridge bowl and nibbled at his shoes even while he was wearing them. At night they climbed up into his bed and played hide-and-seek under the sheets!

The youth released his cat and within two days' time there wasn't a mouse left in the castle. The king was so pleased that he gave the boy one chest filled with gold and another filled with diamonds and other precious jewels.

So it was that the third and youngest of the sons returned home with the largest treasure; and so it was that the three brothers found their fortunes.

The Crane's Revenge
An East Indies Tale

Once upon a time, the long-legged crane sat in his nest and fell into a deep sleep. Soon a family of mischievous monkeys swung down from the nearby trees and amused themselves by pulling the bird's tail feathers out, one by one. Then they screeched and laughed because the crane looked so funny!

The crane awoke and, when he realized what the monkeys had done, began to cry. He couldn't fly without his tail feathers, and if he couldn't fly, he couldn't eat. His mate came to the rescue, however, and during the two long months it took for new feathers to grow, brought him food.

The crane decided that the monkeys should be taught a lesson for being so cruel to him, and he thought and thought about a means of revenge. At last he had a plan and flew up river looking for the old tortoise.

"Friend Tortoise," he exclaimed upon finding him asleep on the muddy river bank, "I need your help. Those mean monkeys have played a terrible trick on me by pulling out my tail feathers, and if it wasn't for my wife, I would have starved to death. Now here is my plan to teach them a good lesson...."

Upon hearing the plan, the tortoise agreed to help. Then he and the crane went in search of an old abandoned row-boat. They found one a short distance away, and the crane proceeded to peck a large hole in the bottom of it.

Then the tortoise crawled under the boat and wedged himself so tightly into the hole with his hard shell that the water could not come in. And with a few flaps of his powerful legs, the tortoise managed to push the boat into the current. The crane stood proudly on the seat, looking like a captain at the ship's helm.

Soon the boat drifted near the tree in which the family of cruel monkeys lived. They saw the crane and called, "Where are you sailing?"

"On an adventure down-river!" replied the crane. "Would you like to join me?"

"Yes!" they chattered, and leaped down out of the tree and into the boat. Now the boat was full and was soon moving rapidly down the river.

"And where will this adventure take us?" asked one of the monkeys.

"Out to the open sea," said the crane. "And just so that you will be safe, I think it best for all of you to tie your tails together. Then the high ocean waves won't be able to toss anyone overboard."

Never having been to sea before, the monkeys thought that the crane's advice was sound and tied their tails tightly together. Soon the boat reached the sea and began to jerk and roll with each wave. The monkeys grew frightened and asked to be taken home, but the crane shouted, "Tortoise, I'm going to fly away now!"

"Very well," said the tortoise from under the boat. "I'll swim on home."

As the crane flapped his wings and lifted into the air, the tortoise popped out of the hole and swam away. The sea rushed in and the boat quickly sank. The monkeys, who by nature are excellent swimmers, had a difficult time staying afloat with their tails tied together. In fact, they very nearly drowned before they made it back to shore.

Then the crane, who was watching from the air, called down to the miserable monkeys, "You got just what you deserved!"

The Astrologer and the Forty Thieves
A Persian Tale

Once there lived an old astrologer in the great city of Ashkabad, in Persia. His name was Jamal and he was an advisor to the king.

Now it so happened that the king's treasury was robbed of forty chests of precious jewels. The captain of the Guard dispatched his troops and the city was thoroughly searched, but to no avail. Then the king sent for Jamal.

"Tell me, old astrologer, who took my jewels?"

Jamal thought for a moment and said, "It was not one man, or even ten, Your Majesty. Rather it was forty—one to carry each chest."

"Excellent," said the king. "Now tell me who they are and where they have hidden the treasure."

"In order to answer you," explained Jamal, "I must have forty days to consult the stars."

"Agreed," said the king, "but if you fail, if the jewels are not returned to my treasury within forty days' time, you will be banished from my court."

Jamal returned home and placed forty figs in a large jar. He planned to take one out each night after his prayers so that he could keep an accurate count of the passing days.

Now, indeed, there were forty thieves, and one of them was an informer at court. When he told his friends that Jamal was able to guess their number, the leader sent one of his men to spy on the astrologer and observe his progress.

He arrived at Jamal's house late that night, just as the old man was finishing his prayers, and listened through a cracked window. Jamal took a fig from the jar and the thief heard him say, "Ah, there is one of the forty."

The thief ran back to the gang and cried, "Jamal has supernatural powers! He can see through walls!"

"Nonsense!" said the leader. "Tomorrow I'll send two of you to keep watch."

The next night two thieves arrived just as Jamal was finishing his prayers. He took a fig from the jar and the scoundrels heard him say, "And now there are two of them."

The frightened thieves ran to tell the others and the following night the leader sent three of his men. The same thing happened that night and the next and the next, until at last, on the fortieth night, all forty thieves were waiting outside Jamal's window.

The astrologer sighed because he hadn't been able to solve the difficult case with his charts and calculations. Then he took the last fig from the jar and said, "The number is complete at last. Now all forty are before me."

The thieves trembled and the leader knocked on Jamal's door. The astrologer was astounded to see forty men file into his house and even more astounded to hear the leader say, "O great and wise man, if you will help to have our lives spared, we will tell you where the king's treasure is hidden."

Jamal went to the king's court the next morning.

"Well, astrologer," said the king, "who has stolen my treasure?"

"Does Your Majesty prefer the thieves or the jewels? The stars above will only tell me one or the other. I cannot give you the answer to both."

"In that case," replied the king, "I choose the treasure."

Jamal consulted his charts as if making a few quick calculations. Then he said, "The treasure will be found in the root cellar of the abandoned estate two miles north of town."

The king was overjoyed to find his jewels and he rewarded Jamal handsomely.

The Three Aunties
A Norwegian Tale

Once long ago, a beautiful orphan girl named Rose knocked on a castle door and asked for work. The queen felt sorry for her and gave her a job in the kitchen. Rose worked hard, but because of her beauty the other kitchen maids became jealous. Thus they told the queen that Rose had bragged that she could spin a pound of flax into fine yarn in twenty-four hours.

"If she says she can do it, then she shall do it," said the queen.

Rose was taken to a room which contained a spinning wheel and the flax and was left all alone. She began to cry because she had never spun before in her life. Just then an ugly old woman with a very long nose came in and asked, "What is wrong, child?"

The lass revealed her problem and the old woman said, "If you promise to call me 'auntie' on your wedding day, I will spin the flax for you."

Rose agreed and then lay down to sleep. When she awoke the next morning, all the flax had been spun into fine yarn. The queen was delighted and that made the kitchen maids even more envious. Thus they told the queen that Rose boasted that she could weave all the yarn into fine cloth in twenty-four hours.

The queen took her to a second room, which contained the yarn and a loom, and wished her good speed. Again Rose began to cry and for a second time she was visited by an ugly old woman, but this one had a large hump on her back. "Why do you cry, pretty one?" she asked.

Rose told her all about it and the old woman said, "If you promise to call me 'auntie' on your wedding day, I'll weave the yarn for you."

The lass promised and then lay down to sleep. When she awoke the next morning, she found that the yarn had been woven into a beautiful piece of linen cloth. The queen was so pleased that she called Rose her favorite servant! The kitchen maids were furious and told the queen that Rose said that she could sew the linen into six shirts within twenty-four hours.

The poor girl was put into a room with a pair of scissors, a needle and thread, and the linen cloth. And again, she started to cry. Before long a third, ugly old woman entered. This one had bright red eyes as large as saucers. Rose told her the reason for her tears and the woman said, "If you will call me 'auntie' on your wedding day, I will sew the shirts for you."

The young girl agreed and then lay down to sleep. When she awoke the next morning, the shirts were made. The queen thought that they were so lovely that she called to her son, the prince, and explained how skilled Rose was at spinning, weaving, and sewing. The prince was charmed by Rose's skills as well as her beauty and asked her to marry him. Rose happily agreed.

A great party was held on the wedding day, and three of the guests were the old women who had helped Rose.

"Good day, my three aunties," said Rose.

"How can they be your aunts?" asked the horrified prince. "You are so beautiful and they are so ugly."

"We were pretty when we were young, too," said the first old woman, "but I got my long nose by sitting at the spinning wheel each day, year after year, and nodding over the whirling yarn."

Then the second old woman spoke up. "I got the hump on my back by bending over the loom each day, year after year."

"And I," said the third woman, "got my red eyes by staring at the tiny stitches as I sewed each day, year after year."

The prince thought for a moment and then said, "From this day forth my bride shall neither spin nor weave nor sew, so that she may always retain her great beauty!"

The Theft of a Smell
A Peruvian Tale

Once upon a time, there lived a stingy baker in the city of Lima, Peru. Early each morning he mixed flour, milk, eggs, and raisins and baked his bread, rolls, and cookies. Then he placed the delicious goods in the open window of his shop and sold them to his customers.

The baker was so stingy that he never gave so much as a crumb of his baked goods away, even if it was a stale crumb and the birds were hungry.

The baker's neighbor, however, was a much different kind of man. He enjoyed a leisurely life and never cared about money or a steady job. In fact, one of his greatest pleasures was smelling the wonderful aromas of the baked goods in the baker's open window. The cool breeze carried the luscious smells to him like a gift each morning. He especially liked the odor of fresh-baked cinnamon rolls.

The selfish baker knew that his neighbor was benefiting from his hard work and he felt that the lazy fellow shouldn't be allowed to have such enjoyment for free. Thus the baker went to his neighbor and said, "You may no longer steal the smell of my baked goods from me. You must pay me ten gold pieces each month for such a privilege. If not, I'll take you to court."

The neighbor laughed and said that it was a good joke! Then he told all the other neighbors about the baker's special smelling fee, and soon the baker was the laughingstock of the city. This made him angry enough to speak to a judge.

The judge had a good sense of humor, and after hearing the complaint, ordered both the baker and the neighbor to appear before him the following day. He also ordered the neighbor to bring ten pieces of gold. The baker was quite pleased to hear this and could already feel the weight of the gold in his pocket.

The next day the courtroom was packed with curious citizens. The judge entered and asked the baker and his neighbor to approach the bench and tell their stories. The baker spoke at length about the beautiful aromas produced by his delicious pastries and how his neighbor had enjoyed them each morning for several years without ever paying so much as a penny for them.

The judge listened patiently to all the baker had to say and then asked the neighbor if he had in fact enjoyed the smells without paying for them. The neighbor replied, "Yes, your honor, it is true."

The judge again spoke to the neighbor, "Take the ten gold pieces from your pocket and shake them in your hand so that we can hear them clink together."

The man was surprised at such a strange request but did as he was told.

"Did you hear the clinking of your neighbor's gold coins?" the judge asked the baker.

"Yes, your honor," said the baker.

"And does the sound of gold coins clinking together please your ears?"

"Yes," replied the baker.

"This, then, is my decision," said the judge. "The neighbor has enjoyed the smell of baked goods. In return, the baker has enjoyed the sound of gold coins. Case dismissed!"

The Baker's Dozen
An American Tale

Long ago, when the town of Albany, New York, was a quaint village in early America, a baker by the name of Van Amsterdam had a successful business. No one in the entire state could bake better tasting cookies, and he sold a big batch each day.

During the Christmas holidays Master Van Amsterdam baked his special cookies. They were shaped like Saint Nicholas, and people came from all over the thirteen colonies to buy them for their holiday feasts. The day before Christmas was especially busy since everyone wanted the baker's wonderful cookies. He worked hard trying to keep up with the orders and was happy when the sun set so that he could finally close his door.

Before he could count the money from the day's sales, however, an ugly old woman banged on the door and demanded to be let in. Van Amsterdam had a few dozen cookies left, so he unlocked the door for her. She wore a patched cloak and a tall peaked hat, and her crooked nose was much too long for her face. She pointed to the cookies shaped like Saint Nicholas and said, "I'll take a dozen."

The baker counted out twelve of the cookies, wrapped them in brown paper, and tied the package with string.

"That's only twelve. I want a dozen. Give me one more!" she demanded.

"I gave you a dozen," said the baker. "A dozen means twelve."

"Twelve plus one more makes a dozen and I want a dozen," she persisted.

"I'm too tired for nonsense," replied the baker. "Everyone knows that a dozen means twelve. Now take the dozen I've given you and leave me alone!"

The old woman began to leave, but turned at the door and said, "You've cheated me out of one cookie and I won't forget it."

During the next week everything went wrong in the bakery. One day Van Amsterdam took a tray full of cookies from the oven and placed them on the counter. A customer came in and said that he wanted all of them, but the baker found it impossible to take them off the tray. Even though he had carefully greased it, the cookies stayed stuck!

On the following day he took another tray of cookies from the oven and watched each cookie carefully slide to the edge of the tray and tumble to the floor. On the next day all of the cookies he baked shrank to one tenth of their original size!

Soon he had nothing to sell, and his customers went to other bakeries. Master Van Amsterdam grew quite worried and prayed to Saint Nicholas for advice.

The kind saint appeared in his dream that night and said, "You are a good baker and have a prosperous business, but I would suggest that you be more generous to others."

The next morning, the old woman was his first customer. "I want a dozen of your best cookies."

The baker quickly counted out thirteen and wrapped them up for her.

She paid him and started to leave, but when she got to the door, she turned and said, "As long as you remain generous, no more trouble will haunt you. Remember that from now on, a baker's dozen is thirteen."

And so it became a custom in the colonies to give an extra measure as a sign of generosity.

The Giant's Bride
A Lapland Tale

Once long ago, when giants roamed the northern section of Scandinavia known as Lapland as freely as the reindeer, a Lapp and his daughter had a close call with a giant. The giants lived in caves, and often the Lapps had to set up camp nearby in order to have an adequate supply of moss for their hungry reindeer.

One day the Lapp and his daughter pitched their tent near the home of a lonely giant. He wasn't especially mean, or even ugly, but just the same, he was a giant and had to be treated with respect.

When the giant came to visit the camp, the Lapp and his daughter were most cordial and invited him to visit again. Unfortunately he came back several times and soon fell in love with the girl. He asked her father's permission to marry her, and the Lapp couldn't very well refuse. But both he and his daughter were miserable, for it was certain that she didn't want such a large and stupid fellow for a husband.

The Lapp was a clever man, and he found many excuses to keep postponing the wedding day. But the giant continued to visit the camp, and with a huge grin on his face, began calling the girl "my little sweetheart."

The father was quite worried. It was obvious that the giant was in love, and if they made him angry, he could eat their reindeer for dinner and both of them for dessert! They had to keep him happy so they made a plan.

The Lapp found a log and carved it into a crude image of his daughter, complete with arms and legs. The girl dressed the life-size doll in her best clothes—a wool dress, a silver belt, and a bright red cap with a heavy veil hanging down over the face. They placed the doll in the tent and then harnessed their strongest reindeer to the sled, which was packed with most of their belongings. The girl crawled into the sled, under the blankets, and her father hid the sled in the trees.

Soon the giant came to the tent and said that it was a good day to be married. The Lapp agreed and invited him inside. The giant greeted his bride by saying, "How pretty you look."

The bride didn't answer.

"My little sweetheart," said the giant, "she's so bashful."

The Lapp wished the giant a happy life with his daughter, showed him that the pot was filled with fresh reindeer meat for the wedding dinner, and then said good-by. He ran to the small clump of trees, jumped onto the sled, and he and his daughter sped away.

"Now, little sweetheart," said the giant who was still in the tent, "put the pot on the fire and cook our dinner."

The bride didn't answer.

"Still bashful? Well, I'll do it myself."

Soon the meat was cooked and the

giant said, "Now it's time to serve the meal."

The bride still didn't answer.

"My little sweetheart, you are *so* bashful. But tell me, are you very hungry?"

The bride still didn't answer.

The giant leaned over and lifted the veil from her face. When he realized that he had married a doll instead of the girl, he was furious! He yelled and stomped on the ground, tore down the tent, and started running after the two Lapps. But he never found them because they had such a long head start, and the new-fallen snow had hidden their tracks.

The Burning of the Rice Fields
A Japanese Tale

Once there was an old man who lived next to the rice fields on the side of a mountain, high above the village and the sea. His grandson lived with him, and together they enjoyed watching over the many rice fields that covered the terraced mountainside.

The rice belonged to everyone in the village and the people climbed the steep and narrow paths that led up to the fields to work each day. The small boy was especially proud that his grandfather was the caretaker, because he realized how important the good rice was to the survival of the villagers.

The grandfather had a habit of getting up early each morning and looking out to sea. He enjoyed watching the sun rise as much as he enjoyed filling his lungs with the crisp salt air.

One morning, however, he saw something unusual happening far beyond the water's edge, out where the sky meets the sea. It looked like a huge green cloud falling into the sea. It also looked like a giant wall of blue water climbing into the sky.

He stared hard at this strange sight for

several long moments. Then he turned and ran into the little cottage and yelled to his sleeping grandchild, "Wake up boy! Bring a blazing stick from the hearth! Hurry! There is no time to lose!"

The boy jumped from his bed and, obeying his grandfather, grabbed a burning stick and ran outside with it. His sleepy eyes opened wide as he saw the old man setting fire to the rice fields.

"Grandfather! What are you doing? Don't burn the precious rice!"

"Quick, boy, use your stick! Burn the fields!" yelled the old man.

With tears rolling down his cheeks, the boy did as he was told. Soon all the fields were ablaze and a heavy black smoke rose to the sky. Some of the villagers below were already up and, seeing the smoke, yelled to awaken the rest of the people. In a few moments everyone was running up the mountainside—men, women, and children alike. No one stayed behind.

But they were too late—the crops were burned beyond all hope.

"How did this happen?" cried the villagers.

"I set the fires," said the old man sadly, "and I made my grandson help."

"But, why?" they demanded angrily. "Why would you do such a thing to us?"

"Look," he said, pointing to the sea.

Everyone looked, but could hardly believe what they saw. A gigantic wall of water, a single wave that reached from the ocean's floor to the sky above came crashing into the village and with a thunderous clap smashed again the base of the mountain! Another wave followed, and another!

Then all was calm once again. The

people were too terrified to speak and could only hold tight to each other and watch as the broken village in which they had been sleeping just minutes before washed out to sea.

The villagers realized that it was the old man's quick thinking that saved them from the tidal wave, and he was honored all the rest of his life.

The Silver Bell
A Danish Tale

Once a young shepherd who was both tired and hungry drove his flock of sheep into a green meadow and found a small silver bell lying in the grass.

He rang the bell and heard the sweet tinkle of a canary's song; or perhaps it was the sound of silver raindrops falling on a broad leaf; or maybe it was the sound of a mother whispering thoughts of love to her newborn child. But the most wonderful thing of all was that upon hearing the tinkling of the bell, the shepherd no longer felt weary or hungry. His heart felt light and his stomach felt full.

"This bell is a treasure!" he exclaimed. "And I will never part with it."

The silver bell actually belonged to one of the dwarfs who lived under the mound at the edge of the meadow. He had been doing somersaults in the grass and the bell fell out of his wee pocket. It was a serious matter because it was the sweet sound of the bell that put him to sleep each night. Thus he began to search for it.

As you know, dwarfs can change their shape by whispering a magic word. First he became a squirrel in order to scamper through the tall grass. Then he became a dog and tried sniffing it out. Soon he changed into a horse so that he could run back and forth across the meadow.

But he had no luck at all. The young shepherd had taken his sheep and the bell over the low hills to another meadow quite some distance away.

Then the dwarf changed himself into a hawk and flew high above the hills until at last he saw the shepherd and his flock. The hawk-dwarf circled lower and lower until he could see the silver bell hanging from a leather thong around the boy's neck.

The hawk landed and the dwarf changed himself into an old woman wearing a ragged dress. She walked up to the shepherd and said, "What a pretty bell you have! And tomorrow is my granddaughter's birthday and I have no gift for her. Would you let me give her your little bell?"

"Oh, I can't give you this bell," explained the youth, "for it is magical. Whenever I ring it the world is filled with sweetness and light! My weariness melts away and my heart fills with gladness! I'm sorry, but I could never part with it."

"Well, I'm much wealthier than I appear to be," said the woman, "and since the little bell charms me so, I'll give you this bag of gold for it." So saying she pulled a large leather bag filled with gold coins from under her shawl.

"I'm sorry," said the boy, "but I won't sell it."

"Then listen carefully, lad, for I am not what I seem. I'm really a witch who practices magic that is white. I can give you a special staff that will bring blessings on your sheep and you will prosper as a shepherd all of your life. Your flock will grow large and you will be the wealthiest shepherd in the land."

"May I see such a stick?" asked the youth in amazement.

The old woman pulled it out from under her shawl. The boy saw that it was made of ivory and had a wonderful carving of the biblical shepherd named David playing his flute while tending his flock.

The boy felt deep in his heart that he could trust this old woman, even though she was strange. "Agreed!" he cried. "The silver bell for the ivory staff."

They made the exchange, and the old woman vanished into thin air. The surprised shepherd failed to notice the hawk that was winging its way home high above him.

"Sleep!" cried the dwarf as soon as he crawled into his bed. "At last I can sleep!"

And the shepherd became a rich and happy man, just as the dwarf had promised.

Two Wives
An East Indian Tale

Once there was a man who had the great misfortune of marrying two wives. He soon learned that if he wanted to keep peace in the family, he could not favor one more than the other.

One quiet afternoon, all three were sitting in the garden, resting from the heat of the midday sun. One of the wives was combing her husband's black hair and saw a single white one. She quickly yanked it out.

"Ow!" cried the man. "What are you doing?"

"I found a white hair and pulled it out," said the first wife.

The second wife spoke up and said, "Foolish woman! A white hair is the sign of approaching wisdom. How dare you pull it out!"

"If it is a sign of wisdom," explained the first wife, "I shall keep it with me always."

"It is not right," complained the second wife, "that you should have a hair while I have none!"

The husband tried to stop the argument by saying, "Dear wives of mine, please don't argue. It is only fair that since my first wife found the white hair, it shall be hers to keep. And it is only fair that since my second wife has none, she shall pull out one of my black hairs. Then each of you will have one."

As soon as the second wife yanked out a black hair, the first wife said, "But husband, she has a black one and mine is white. I, too, want a black one."

"Very well," said the man. "Pull a black hair from my head and be satisfied."

As soon as she plucked the hair, the second wife said angrily, "But she has both a black and a white hair. I have only one black. It isn't fair!"

"You are quite right, my dearest," said the husband. "Simply pull one more hair from my head and you will each have two."

That made the first wife even more jealous. "Now she has two black hairs and I have only one. It is not right, husband, for you to love her more than you love me."

"I'm sorry, sweet wife," said the man whose head was beginning to hurt. "You must take another black one."

Then the second wife screamed, "She has three hairs and I have two! I want three as well!"

"Yes, yes, you may take one more, my dearest," said the poor man.

But of course that dissatisfied the first wife and she had to have another hair. And to keep peace the husband had to give the second wife yet another.

The argument lasted all afternoon with both wives yanking the hairs from his head until as last he was completely bald!

Even though the poor man's head

ached, he smiled happily, for now the argument was over and both of his wives were silent.

Red Cap and the Miser
An Irish Tale

Once there was a stingy old Irishman named Phillip. He was so stingy, in fact, that his neighbors said he had sold his hair to the leprechauns for pillow stuffing and that was why his head was as bald as a hard-boiled egg.

It wasn't like Phillip to give anything away, and when he discovered that a bit of fresh milk was missing from the big milk can in the barn, he was furious. "I'll catch the thief and he will pay double—no, triple, for what he took! You just wait and see, Annie!"

Annie was his wife and she had listened to his rantings for many a long year. "Ah, to be sure, it's but a wee bit that's gone. We'll hardly miss it."

"Nobody takes my milk without paying for it!" shouted Phillip, "Tonight I'll hide in the barn and catch me a thief, that I will!"

He was hiding behind a large pile of hay when Red Cap, the leprechaun, walked up to the milk can with a tiny pail in hand. Phillip stepped out in front of him, startling the wee fellow, and said with an angry sneer, "I've caught you red-handed, you little sneak! What do you say to that?"

"I say that you're an old miser, Phillip, and a grouch as well! You're always complaining that my thorn tree grows too close to your corn field, and now you accuse me of stealing your milk. Your father always gave me a little milk, and your grandfather did too, but not you. You want to be paid. Well how much is it that I owe you?"

"I want gold for all the milk you've taken from me and from my father and from his father too. I also want back payment for all the years that you've lived under the thorn tree. And if you don't pay me fairly, I'll cut the tree down and grow corn there instead."

Suddenly the leprechaun yanked his red cap from his head and tossed it high into the air. Plop! It landed on Phillip's bald head, and there it stayed. He pulled and tugged and jerked, but it wouldn't budge an inch.

"You want payment, do you?" asked Red Cap. "You want to cut down me thorn tree, do you? You want to grow corn in its place, do you? Well, I'll give you corn, I will!"

And so saying, he skipped out the barn door in the wink of an eye.

Phillip went back into the house wearing the red cap. His wife pulled with all her strength, but still it wouldn't come off, and he had to wear it to bed. The next morning, however, he felt something growing under the cap. "It's hair, Annie! That thieving leprechaun has given me hair back!"

Annie used her scissors to split a seam and look inside the cap. "If it's hair then it's green, and little ears are growing on the stalks. It's corn that you're growing, husband, not hair."

"I'm bewitched!" cried Phillip. "That old leprechaun has won. Get me a dozen eggs and a pound of sweet butter, Annie, and I'll go apologize."

"Red Cap," he called when he got to the thorn tree, "please take these gifts, and you can have all the milk you want from now on. Just please take the cap off my head, and the corn too."

"Will you put a nice fence around my tree, and bring me a bit of cheese each week?" asked the leprechaun from under the tree. He missed his cap, and besides, he had played his joke and had some fun.

"Yes," said Phillip, "whatever you say."

"Agreed," said the leprechaun and the cap flew off the man's head. He felt his scalp and found that it was as bald as before. Greatly relieved, Phillip went on home, and from that time forth, he tried to be nice to everyone.

The Old Man With a Wart
A Japanese Tale

Once there was an old man who had a large wart on the right side of his face. It was so large that it looked like a ripe peach growing on his cheek! It made him look rather funny, but he did not complain.

One day, while up in the mountains, he got caught in a terrible storm. The wind howled and the trees groaned. Lightning flashed across the sky and a torrent of rain began to fall. The old man found a hollow tree and climbed inside. Here was a cozy shelter in which to wait for the storm to end.

Soon, however, he heard the voices of strangers coming toward him. They were happy voices, full of laughter and song, but they also sounded like the shrill winds and the swaying of trees in the storm.

When the strangers arrived near the tree in which the old man hid, they began to build a large bonfire. In the light of the flames, the old man saw that his companions were giants with great wings folded on their backs. They were the Storm Spirits!

The old man shivered in fear and

then, because he was cold and wet, sneezed loudly. The Storm Spirits heard him and dragged him from the tree.

"Dance!" they demanded with windy voices. "Dance around the fire as we sing in the rain."

The old man loved to dance and he began to turn round and round, bending like a flower in the storm and leaping high into the air like a deer in flight.

Soon the song of the spirits grew soft and sweet and the man started to sway like an old pine in a gentle breeze. At last the song ended and the man sat down to rest. The rain stopped falling and the sun peeked through the clouds.

"Wonderful!" cried the Storm Spirits. "You must come tomorrow and dance for us again. And to make sure that you will be here, we will take this beautiful peach that grows on your face away from you.

But do not worry—we will give it back to you tomorrow."

They took his wart and let him go home.

When he arrived in the village, all the people asked what had happened to his wart, and the old man told them the whole story.

One of the old man's neighbors was of nearly the same age and also had a large wart, but his was on the left side of his face. This neighbor decided that he would pay a visit to the Storm Spirits the following day and get them to take his wart away, too. Thus he climbed the mountain and hid in the hollow tree, waiting for the Spirits to arrive.

Soon the storm hit and, oh, it was fierce! The lightning tore holes in the sky and the rain fell like fury. The old man grew afraid. It wasn't long before the

Storm Spirits arrived and built their fire. Then they found the man in the tree and dragged him out. "Dance!" they demanded. "Dance for us like you did yesterday."

But he was too scared to dance and could only stand before them, trembling like a frightened rabbit. That made the Spirits angry and they said, "If you can't dance any better than that, we don't want you to be with us. Take your peach and go home!"

Thus they put the first old man's wart on the right side of the second man's face and made him run down the mountainside. The poor old man had to live out his remaining years with large warts on both cheeks instead of just one.

Señor Coyote, the Judge
A Mexican Tale

Once Señor Rattlesnake was taking his afternoon nap out on the hot sand next to the hole that led down to his cool nest. Suddenly a large stone came rolling down the mountainside and landed on top of him. He wiggled and squirmed and pushed and rolled, but it was no use. He was hopelessly pinned to the ground.

Soon Señor Rabbit hopped by. "Good afternoon, Señor Rattlesnake. I see that you are carrying a heavy rock on your back. Are you planning to build a stone house?"

"Please don't tease me, amigo," said the rattlesnake. "This cruel stone is hurting me and I need your help. Lift it off of me and I will reward you handsomely."

The rabbit had a kind heart and hated to see anyone suffer. Thus he sat on the ground next to the snake and pushed on the stone with his big feet. He pushed hard, and then harder, and even harder! At last the stone shifted and Señor Rattlesnake was free.

"You did well, Señor Rabbit," said the snake. "And now I will reward you."

"Oh, it was nothing," said the tired rabbit. "I don't deserve anything in return."

"Yes-s-s you do," hissed Señor Rattlesnake, and he began to coil.

"What are you doing?" cried the rabbit. "I just saved you life."

"Yes-s-s, I'm going to eat you, and that will be your reward."

Señor Rattlesnake prepared to strike. The rabbit was too frightened to run and merely stood there, shaking all over.

Just then Señor Coyote walked by. "What is the meaning of this?" he asked.

The snake started to speak and so did the rabbit. Each wanted to tell his side of the story.

"Wait!" said Señor Coyote. "Tell your stories one at a time and I will be the judge. Señor Rabbit, you will be first."

"I found Señor Rattlesnake trapped under the stone. He asked me for help and I pushed it off of him. Then he said he was going to reward me by making me his dinner."

"No, no!" cried the snake. "Señor Rabbit has it all wrong. I crawled under the stone to get out of the hot sun. I could have crawled back out whenever I wanted. I just played a little trick on the rabbit so that I could have him for my dinner."

Señor Coyote looked very serious as he thought about his decision and then asked, "Do you both agree that Señor Rattlesnake was under the stone?"

They both nodded their heads to say "yes."

"In that case," said the coyote, "I want Señor Rattlesnake to crawl back under the stone so that I can see just how everything was. Then I can judge this difficult case fairly."

Señor Rattlesnake thought quickly

and said, "But now that Señor Rabbit has moved the stone, I can no longer crawl under it. You two will have to roll it on me."

Señor Coyote and Señor Rabbit agreed and rolled the heavy stone on top of Señor Rattlesnake.

"Is that just the way you were?" asked the coyote?

"Yes-s-s," hissed the snake. "Now hurry and get this stone off of me!"

"I have a better idea," explained Señor Coyote. "You will stay right where you are, and that will be *your* reward for being unkind to the one who tried to help you. Good day, Señor Rattlesnake."

Notes

Although not a folklorist, I'm a storyteller with a true appreciation of folklore. The tales in this collection have come to me from both the written and oral traditions. My tellings are the product of more than twenty years of sharing them aloud. Whenever possible, I've researched the origins of the stories as well as the ways in which they have been adapted by different cultures. Even though I haven't always succeeded in tracing the origins, I trust that you will discover something of value herein.

Motifs given (where appropriate) are from Margaret Read MacDonald, *The Storyteller's Sourcebook: A Subject, Title and Motif Index to Folklore Collections for Children.* (Detroit: Neal-Schuman/Gale, 1982).

The Extraordinary Cat
China, page 9

Motif L392.0.4. I often introduce this tale by asking my listeners for the names of their cats. In the telling, I emphasize the line, "The children were the wisest of all..." And it is the children who invariably end the story for me by saying, the name is "CAT!"

For a Vietnamese version, see *The Toad is the Emperor's Uncle: Animal Folktales from Viet-Nam* by Vo-Dinh (Garden City, New York: Doubleday, 1970), pp. 123-28.

The Proud Fox

United States, page 19

Motif J2351.1, Type 154. I ask my listeners to define the word "pride," before telling this story. The responses are wide and varied. One second grade boy said it was the name of his breakfast cereal. After the story I ask again. The insightfulness of their responses is always impressive.

For a European version, see *European Folk and Fairy Tales* by Joseph Jacobs (New York: Putnam, 1916, 1967), pp. 42-50.

The Wisdom of Solomon

Israel, page 23

Motif H540.2.1. This beautiful story demonstrates, once again, how easy it is to teach without effort. I often use it in business settings when problem solving is an issue.

For an earlier version, see *Once Upon a Time Stories* by Rose Dobbs (New York: Random, 1950), pp. 19-23.

The Bear Who Said North

Finland, page 27

Motif K561.1.0.5. A great story for facial expressions! Clench your teeth and draw out the last word: "Eeeeeeaassssst!"

For another version, see *Tales From a Finnish Tuppa* by James Cloyd Bowman and Margery Bianco (Chicago: Albert Whitman, 1936, 1965), p. 257.

Toads and Diamonds

France, page 31

Motif D1554.2. The Cinderella story has more variations than any other fairy tale. In this version, listeners particularly enjoy the revenge on the sister.

For a traditional version, see *The Blue Fairy Book* by Andrew Lang (New York: Longmans, Green, 1929), pp. 295-98.

The Shoemaker's Dream

Holland, page 35

Motif N531.1.1. With the proliferation of state lotteries, I ask my listeners if they have ever dreamed of winning the big prize. "What if," I then ask, "you dreamed four of the six numbers? How would you obtain the other two?" Then I tell this tale.

For another simple telling, see *Tricky Peik and Other Picture Tales* by Jeanne B. Hardendorff (Philadelphia: Lippincott, 1967), pp. 33-9.

The Bat

Central Asia (Mongolia), page 39

Motif B261.1.0.3. Even very young listeners seem to empathize with the bat's desire to escape the tax collector. This story originated in the Altai mountain region of Central Asia.

For another telling, see *More Tales of Faraway Folk* by Babette Deutsh and Avrahm Yarmolinsky (New York: Harper & Row, 1963), pp. 7-10.

The Seven Stars

Native American (Cherokee), page 43

Motif A773.4.1. Because this plot moves forward so rapidly and contains a surprising and expansive ending, it is rewarding to tell. In the Brazilian Amazon variation, the oldest of seven brothers leads his six siblings into the sky to become the Pleiades.

For another Cherokee version, see *American Indian Tales and Legends* by Vladimir Hulpach (New York: Hamlyn, 1965), pp. 43-5.

Josesito the Goat

South America, 47

Motif K1715.3.0.2. In South American legend, Cabrakan is the name of a boastful earth giant strong enough to heave mountains into the air. It is a fitting name for the boastful leopard.

For another version, see *The Frog's Saddle Horse and Other Tales* by Jeanne B. Hardendorff (Philadelphia: Lippincott, 1968), pp. 75-82.

Three Children of Fortune

Europe, page 51

Motif N411.1.B. The inheritance of a cat often brings good fortune in folk literature. Perhaps the key story is "Puss and Boots."

The French version of my telling is found in Animal Stories by Walter De La Mare (New York: Scribner's, 1940), pp. 128-32.

The Crane's Revenge

East Indies, page 55

Motif K1040. By playing helper as well as trickster, Tortoise expands his usual role. After the telling, it is the primary children who usually say, "Those monkeys deserved it!"

In a Persian variation, Stork takes revenge on Fox for eating her young. See *Persian Folk and Fairy Tales* by Anne Sinclair Mehdevi (New York: Knopf, 1970), pp. 44-50.

The Astrologer and the Forty Thieves

Persia, page 59

Motif N611.5. Long ago in Persia, the terms "astrologer" and "astronomer" were interchangeable. I particularly like the astrologer's generous treatment of the thieves.

For another version, see *Rumanian Folk Tales* by Jean Ure (New York: Watts, 1960, 1961), pp. 26-32.

The Three Aunties

Norway, page 63

Motif D2183.1. Rose's power to attract the aunties must come from her inner beauty. A good question for your listeners after the telling is, "Why did the other kitchen maids fear her beauty?"

For a Danish version, see *The Golden Lynx* by Augusta Baker (Philadelphia: Lippincott, 1960), pp. 41-5.

The Theft of a Smell

Peru, page 67

Motif J1172.2.0.1. The day I actually brought a dozen fresh-baked cinnamon rolls and a handful of quarters to the telling was the most successful of all.

I first discovered this story in *Folktales of Latin America* by Shirlee Newman (Indianapolis: Bobbs-Merrill, 1962), pp. 19-26.

The Baker's Dozen

United States, page 71

Motif V429.2. This tale makes an interesting addition to Christmas programs. It also provides an unusual introduction to colonial history.

For another version, see *With a Wig, With a Wag, and Other American Folk Tales* by Jean Cothran (New York: McKay, 1954), pp. 18-22.

The Giant's Bride

Lapland, page 75

Motif G561.2.D. Once again, the cruel and stupid giant is defeated through cleverness. I've always found that children bond instantly with the father and daughter in this tale. Few are sympathetic to the beast.

For a German variation, see *Household Stories* by Jakob Ludwig Karl Grimm and Wilhelm Karl Grimm (New York: McGraw-Hill, 1886, 1966), pp. 1-2.

The Burning of the Rice Field

Japan, page 79

Motif J1688. This popular Japanese story is as potentially powerful in the telling as the wave itself. When Grandfather points to the sea and says, "Look...," actually see the wave in your mind's eye. The effect on your listeners will be impressive.

For another telling, see *The Wave* by Margaret Hodges (Boston: Houghton Mifflin, 1964).

The Silver Bell
Denmark, page 83

Motif P451.5.1.5.0.3. Dwarfs are much more generous than leprechauns. Here, listeners seem to enjoy the dwarf's transformations as much as the plot.

I discovered this tale in *A Book of Dwarfs* by Ruth Manning-Sanders (New York: Dutton, 1963), pp. 89-94.

Two Wives
India, page 87

Motif J2112.2. Before telling this story, I explain how marriage customs have culturally differed throughout history. During the telling I amplify the wives' power by playing their roles to the hilt. It always produces welcome laughter!

For another version, see *Noodlehead Stories From Around the World* by Moritz A. Jagendorf (New York: Vanguard, 1957) pp. 24-9.

Red Cap and the Miser
Ireland, page 91

Leprechauns are powerful warriors who usually win in the end. I heard this story from an Irish immigrant who spoke with a rich brogue. I had to ask him for clarification throughout the telling. It appears to be more fiction than folk tale, and is thus difficult to trace.

The Old Man With a Wart

Japan, page 95

Motif F344.1.2. This is a wonderful tale for classroom enactment. You play narrator and select two boys or girls for the old-folk's roles. Everyone else plays the Storm Spirits. Trust the children to create an entertaining dance.

I discovered this tale in *Fairy Tales of the Orient* by Pearl S. Buck (New York: Simon & Schuster, 1965), pp. 232-36.

Señor Coyote, the Judge

Mexico, page 99

Motif J1172.3. This story appeals to children's innate sense of fair play. Have fun playing up Señor Rattlesnake's superiority.

For another version, see *The Buried Treasure and Other Picture Tales* by Eulalie Steinmetz Ross (Philadelphia: Lippincott, 1958), pp. 89-94.

Other Books From August House Publishers

Thirty-Three Multicultural Tales to Tell

Stories from many cultures collected and presented in concise, "retellable" form by Pleasant DeSpain.

Hardback $25.00 / ISBN 0-87483-265-9
Paperback $15.00 / ISBN 0-87483-266-7

Barking at a Fox-Fur Coat

Family stories and tall tales by renowned storyteller Donald Davis. "His stories left listeners limp with laughter at the same time they struggled with a lump in their throat."—Wilma Dykeman, *New York Times*

Hardback $19.95 / ISBN 0-87483-141-5
Paperback $9.95 / ISBN 0-87483-140-7

Rachel the Clever

and Other Jewish Folktales

Forty-six tales brought to America by immigrants from countries and regions as diverse as the stories. Collected and retold by Josepha Sherman.

Hardback $18.95 / ISBN 0-87483-306-X
Paperback $11.95 / ISBN 0-87483-307-8

African-American Folktales

Stories from the black oral tradition that transcend color and culture collected and edited by Richard and Judy Dockrey Young.

Hardback $18.95 / ISBN 0-87483-308-6
Paperback $9.95 / ISBN 0-87483-309-4

White Wolf Woman

and Other Native American Transformation Myths

More than forty myths from the oral traditions of thirty Native American tribes in which heros and heroines transform themselves into snakes, birds, bears, wolves, and everyday objects. Collected and retold by Teresa Pijoan.

Hardback $17.95 / ISBN 0-87483-201-2
Paperback $8.95 / ISBN 0-87483-200-4

August House Publishers
P.O. Box 3223, Little Rock, Arkansas 72203
1-800-284-8784